UNCLE SAM'S KIDS

MOVING AGAIN MOM

WRITTEN BY ANGELA SPORTELLI-REHAK
ILLUSTRATED BY GREGG HINLICKY

AN ABIDENME BOOK

Copyright 2004
Abidenme Books
Post Office Box 144
Island Heights, New Jersey 08732-0144 USA

With special thanks to Gregg, for transforming my visions into beautiful illustrations,
all my family and friends, near and far, "who live in my heart," and Jeanette for going "above and beyond."

First Printing 2004
Text and Illustrations Copyright 2004© Angela Sportelli-Rehak
Printed in the United States of America

Publisher's Cataloging in Publication Data
Sportelli-Rehak, Angela.
Moving Again Mom / written by Angela Sportelli- Rehak;
Illustrated by Gregg Hinlicky.
p.cm.--(Uncle Sam's Kids)
SUMMARY: Daddy's new job means moving, and Lil'M
is sad about leaving her best friend.
Audience: Grades K-5
ISBN 0-9714515-2-4
[1.Moving, Household--Juvenile fiction. 2. Children of
military personnel--Juvenile fiction. 3. United
States--Armed Forces--Military life-- Fiction.]
I. Hinlicky, Gregg. II. Title.

PZ7.S76386Mov 2004
[Fic]QBI33-2020
LCCN 2004106575

Dedication

For my husband, whose enthusiasm is contagious;

without you "Uncle Sam's Kids" would be just a dream.

For my mother, whose creativity inspired"Uncle Sams Kids"name.

And in memory of Pop, who taught us how to take one day at a time

and enjoy the journey.

"Don't forget to see the Grand Canyon and the Painted Desert!"

Pat you will always be my shining star...

It was the day before the big move to the West Coast!

"Daddy got a new job and we get to move to a new base!" said Mommy.

"I don't want to move again, Mom!" cried Lil'M. "I like this base and all my friends who live here!"

"I know," said Mommy. "But you are one of Uncle Sam's Kids, and when it's time to move again, we go."

Lil'M ran up to her room and slammed the door.

The next morning Lil'M woke up early. She didn't see her sister, Breezy, in the bed next to her. "Mommy, where did Breezy go?" she asked.

"She went with Daddy to the store to buy a mop. We have to leave everything nice and clean for the next family who will move in here. So, rise and shine," said Mommy with a smile. "We've got to start scrubbing!"

"Ding Dong!"

Nick raced Lil'M to the front door. He was greeted by two moving men. One was a jolly man with a curly, black moustache, and the other was a tall man who had dazzling red hair.

"Good morning," chuckled the man with the moustache, "we're here to move your quarters."

Lil'M tugged at Mommy. "Can I have some quarters too?" she pleaded.

Mommy smiled and said, "No honey, quarters means a house on base. But, if you help me finish packing, I'll give you a few quarters that you can spend!"

"Well, we're all packed," said Mommy with a sigh. "But, wait, where's Lil'M?" She asked.

"I bet I know where she is," said Breezy.

Then in a flash, Breezy ran to the tunnel where they used to play and found Lil'M crying.

"Why are you crying?" Breezy whispered.

"I-I don't want to move. I will miss Kim Lin. She's my best friend," cried Lil'M.

"Don't be sad," Breezy said. "You'll see, you'll make lots of new friends. Besides, moving can be fun! Come on, we have to go now."

Breezy then took her sister by the hand, and they walked back to Mommy.

When Lil'M saw Mommy, she ran into her arms and cried. "Kim Lin and I can't be friends anymore!"

Mommy hugged her and said, "that just isn't true. When you make a real friend, that friend lives in your heart wherever you go. Even though you'll make new friends, you'll still keep your old ones."

"Moving can be a lot of fun," said Mommy.

"Why?" sniffed Lil'M.

"You'll get to see new places and make new friends" she said.

"I don't want to see any new places, or make new friends," said Lil'M, as two tears rolled down her cheek.

Just then, Kim Lin and her mother came to their back gate. Lil'M was so happy to see them. She quickly dried her tears.

"Hi Lil'M," said Kim Lin.

"Hi girls," said Kim Lin's mother.

They both waved their hands high up in the air. Kim Lin's mom held two small boxes in her hand. Each box was specially wrapped. One had red and white stripes, with a bright blue ribbon on it. The other had blue and white stars, with an orange ribbon around it.

"Girls, I brought both of you special moving gifts," said Kim Lin's mom, "you can open them now."

"Wow," said Lil'M, as she opened her box.

"It's a pen with Kim Lin's picture on it!"

"Look!" said Kim Lin. "Mine has Lil'M's picture on it!"

Kim Lin's mother then smiled and said, "These best friend pens will help you both to be brave and happy as you meet new people, and discover new places. But, they can only help you if you believe in the strength of your friendship."

"I'll write to you always," said Lil'M.

"Me too," said Kim Lin.

"We're off!" announced Daddy.
"Can I give Lil'M and Nick the star pads we got at the store this morning, asked Breezy. Mommy corrected her and said "you mean may I." Daddy said, "Sure," he grinned. "Kids, I bought these so you can write about what you learn on our trip. Always be proud of what we do for our country, even if that means moving to the West Coast!"
They all laughed, but Lil'M still felt sad.

The first day, they drove through the lush green Shenandoah Valley. They went up and down lots of high hills. "Mommy, hold on to my blankie," said Lil'M. Lil'M missed Kim Lin. "I know!" she thought. "I will draw her a picture with my best friend pen."

Day two, they stopped at a theme park in the Smokey Mountains of Tennessee. Nick couldn't wait to ride on the big black steam engine. It chugged the whole way up a tall mountain, and through the thick woods.

On the third day, they arrived in Memphis, Tennessee. Mommy couldn't wait to see where the "king of rock and roll" once lived! She took a picture of the big iron gates in front of where he had lived. They were made to look like music notes.

The fourth day, they went to Oklahoma. "Look at the brown and white cows!" Breezy shouted. "Can we take a picture?" "Ok," said Daddy, as he drove the car to the cow pen. They all got out and Mommy took their picture. "Ok, say *moo*," she said with a chuckle.

The fifth and sixth days, they drove through New Mexico. Everyone had lots of time to think. Mommy and Daddy talked about all the unpacking they would do. They wondered how long it would take them to finish.

Nick dreamed about his favorite sport, soccer. "I hope my school has a team," he thought. "I wonder if they have an all-star team? I hope they need a goalie."

What would Breezy's room look like? "A red comforter and a red rug on the floor would be cool," she thought. She couldn't wait to sleep in her very own canopy bed, and on her own soft, fluffy pillows.

Lil'M wondered, "Will there be a playground in my backyard?" Would she find a friend who liked to play on the swings as much as she and Kim Lin did?

On the seventh day of their trip they went to the Grand Canyon in Arizona. The sun was just starting to set.

Breezy jumped up and down and shouted, "Look at all the rims changing colors. You can see red, orange, and even some purple!"

"It looks just like the postcard we got at the rest stop," said Lil'M.

Daddy took their picture and said "Behold, one of the Seven Wonders of the World!"

"Wow!" said Nick. "Look at how far you can see from up here!"

Everyone had a great time at the Grand Canyon. By now it was the eighth day of their trip. They couldn't wait to get to California, so Daddy drove all night until they finally arrived! The guards at the gate greeted them with a salute.

"Cool," said Nick. "Look at the fighter jet!"

"Listen," Mommy said. "We have to wait a few hours until we can move into our new quarters. Why don't we all put on our bathing suits, and go over to the pool!"

"Will there be other kids at the pool?" asked Lil'M.

"You bet," Mommy said.

"Yeah!" they all shouted.

Once they arrived, Lil'M looked through the gate at all the children in the pool. She clutched her hands on the top of the pool gate and worried. "What if nobody likes me? My tummy feels like there are butterflies in it. I wish Kim Lin were here."

"What if I can't make friends?" she said.

"I'm sure you'll make friends," said Nick. "Anyway, I'm sure they all felt like you do when they first moved here and had to meet new people. Don't forget, Lil'M, they are all Uncle Sam's Kids, just like us."

"C'mon," said Breezy, "Let's jump in. It's so hot!"

Lil'M thought about what Mommy had said. "You can make new friends and still keep the old ones ." Then, it all made sense to her! It's not the pen that brings us the strength to make new friends, but the strength inside each one of us. That's what Kim Lin's mom meant when she said, "these pens can only help you if you believe in the strength of your friendship." Lil'M thought, "I know Kim Lin and I will always be friends." She had a burst of courage, and said to Nick and Breezy, "I am going to make new friends!"

"Cool!" said Nick.

"Let's go," said Breezy,

Lil'M walked with both of them to the pool.

Lil'M held her nose and jumped feet first into the pool. "Splash!" She swam to the top. There was a girl who looked like she was having a lot of fun swimming right next to her.

"Hi," said Lil'M with a brave smile. "I just moved here. My name is Lil'M, what's yours?"

"Hi, I'm Juanita," replied the girl, "but all my friends call me Nita."

Lil'M thought, "She wants me to call her Nita and that's what all her friends call her. I hope this mean she wants to be my friend."

"Let's go Lil'M, it's time to move into our new home," said Daddy.

"Can Nita come with us?" she pleaded.

"Not today, we have a lot of unpacking to do," he replied. "But once we're all settled Juanita, you can come to our house to play. We have a big playground right in our backyard."

"Thank you, Sir," said Juanita.

"Oh good," said Lil'M. "We can play on the swings. Then, when we're done we can go in my room and draw pictures with my best friend pen."

"Okay," said Juanita.

"Bye," said Lil'M.

"Bye," said Juanita.

"Home sweet home!" said Mommy as she stood in front of their new house. She couldn't wait to unpack all her treasures, and find them a special place in each room. Daddy was so happy to be in the sunshine. He loved the palm trees in their front yard. Nick just wanted to find his soccer ball. Breezy was so eager to unpack her red comforter.

But all Lil'M wanted was to use her best friend pen, and write to Kim Lin.

From that day on, Lil'M always used her best friend pen. The best friend pen was special because it reminded her that it was the strength of her friendship with Kim Lin that helped her to be brave. It was that same strength that helped her to make her own choices. She learned that her choice to be happy brought her to new places and new friends. Lil'M smiled and looked up at Mommy from under the covers and asked, "When are we moving again, Mom?" and they both laughed.